THE JUDAS

POEMS

MARY BLAKE

THE LITTORAL PRESS

First published in 2007 by:
The Littoral Press 38 Barringtons,
10 Sutton Road, Southend-on-Sea,
Essex SS2 5NA

ISBN 978-0-9550926-6-4

© Mary Blake 2007

British Library Cataloguing-in-Publication Data:
A catalogue record of this book is available from the British Library

All rights reserved

Printed by 4edge Ltd. Hockley. www.4edge.co.uk

Some of these poems were published in 'Littoral', 'The Shop' and various Ver Poet's anthologies.

'Moon Trap, won 1st prize in 'John Cotton's 10 Liners' 2006 and 'Summer was a Cabin by the Sea' won 2nd prize in the same competition in 2000.

'In Silence I found Her' was published in 'Circles of Silence' 'Barton, Longman & Todd.'

"The stream of creation and dissolution never stops…
All things come out of the one, and the one out of all things."

Heraclitus. Circa 500 B.C.

CONTENTS

Wild Garlic	7
Waiting Out	8
Dark as an Old Mercury Backed Mirror	9
Fishing	10
Some Functions of a Rose	11
It Does not Do	12
Moon Trap	13
The Box	14
In the Wood	15
Midsummer Dance	16
Flora and Fauna	17
Fred	18
Cat	19
The Judas Deer	20
Moon Struck	21
Rana Temporaria	22
Three	24
Water Lily	25
Dendrocopus major - The Great Spotted	26
Interweaving	27
Outing	28
Underwater	30
After e e cummings	31
Remembering	32
Holly Trees	33
Poplars	34
Like teeth in a Skull	35
Midsummer's Eve	36
Consider the Lilies of the Field	37
A Chaplet	38
Lady in the Straw	39
Earth	40
One of the Graeae	41
Out of Tune	42
Kalends	43
Finding Love	55

Shape Shifter	56
Trees	57
Ringshall	58
Wheeler End	59
Tobias had his Angel	60
Swiftly Comes the Sparrowhawk	61
Third Hand	62
Winter Afternoon	64
Early Morning	65
Fog	66
Winter	67
Forecast	68
Summer	69
Change	70
Yesterday	71
Gravel Gardens	72
Post Card from the Abyss	73
December 2nd 1984	74
Le Chat Blanc	75
Helix Aspersa	76
A Proliferation of pigs	77
Gardening for Words	78
Hobby Horse	79
A Wood in Late November	80
Green Garlands	82
Green Man	83
A Cottage Garden	84
In Silence I Found Her	85
Peeling an Onion	86
May Morning	90
St Brendan's Rowing Boat	91
Blue Tit	92

WILD GARLIC

West wind blows strong
blows through the woods
scents the air
with wild garlic

a delicate flower
umbels of six petalled stars
open from pearls
held by slender stalks

three in one and one in three
a biretta of green seeds
at its centre, white flowers
lighting the forest floor

threading as a stream
winding its way
through unfurling fronds
of bracken, stiff cobras

sentinels at attention
heads bowed
in astonishment
of wild garlic.

WAITING OUT

The sun has gulped
the cool from the dawn,
roses droop, their first flush
limp and forlorn

I find refuge in the barn
dark, cobwebbed, smelling of mould
waiting out,　　　as a boat waits
for the tide to change, for deep waters
when breathing comes easy.

DARK AS AN OLD MECURY BACKED MIRROR

a pool under willow, willow above, willow below
look down, not to the sky, down
where fishes cause ever widening circles,
circles of stillness, a land of rushes, of reeds
of shuttlecock ferns taller than a child,
reflections clearer in water than air
willow branches, a young girl's floating hair
small steps into forgetfulness…

FISHING

I heard reeds swaying
smelt salt on the air
heard water lapping

almost I had it,
a blue fish floundering
sparkling with water, netted.

Foolishly I let it go, went
into the garden to weed, to hoe, forgot
the poem in my head

instead, I watched a fat red worm wriggle
deep into moist earth, a song-thrush smash
       a silver snail on an anvil of flint.

SOME FUNCTIONS OF A ROSE

To scent the air
          to deck a bride
strew upon a marriage bed
          to cure a mad dog
to make a tisane
          to fill a still room
to cure the plague
          to make a Tussy Mussy
to touch
          petals softer than a baby's caul
or young child's skin
          crowns to place on virgins' coffins
to scent a vault.

IT DOES NOT DO...

to look too closely
looks that swallow
whole the other,
fingers brushing
touching, crushing

it does not do
to peer too closely
eyes grow denser
dark as poppies
slender shadows
sensing strangers
dissolve, dissemble
it does not do
to stare,

this is the way
to the garden
where cuckoo-pint
is bruised
love-lies-bleeding
wormwood
spikes the air.

MOON TRAP

It happens too suddenly
the clock's ticking too quickly
yesterday has toppled, fallen
far too far for me to reach

the little girl dressing up
the big girl undressing
lovers, babies, heartache growing

more often now the moon is caught
tangled in the apple tree
tell me, is there some other way
to set it free?

Turn around and life is passing
dust on the window dust on the chair
wipe all the panes of glass
now watch   the stars grow near…

THE BOX

So easy to forget
the baggage children carry
packed layer upon layer
protected by tissue paper.

Think how birds become silent
with the sparrowhawk in the air.

Tissue paper is very thin
crumples as did my mother.

For a child, when a grown up
falls in a heap, the sky falls.

A crowd soon came
moon faces staring down on us,
me trying to pull her up,
she not moving.

Fear,
coldness so deep inside
the first steps in dying.

Now you wait
for the next time and the next
guilt you never understand
never goes away.

You learn to shoulder pain
it is the box you begin to pack.

Your world shrinking,
the path outside
soiled in feathers
a broken nest,
sparrowhawks drop from nowhere.

IN THE WOOD

It was so sudden
He jumped across my path
He was so quick
He was the colour of bracken
With the sun glinting on it
He was the arch of a rainbow
There, across my path
Then he was gone
The young fox.

MIDSUMMER DANCE

It was the sound
it rent the air
the saddest, most haunting cry I know
sadder than waves breaking on rocks,
the cry of peacocks.

So many
some roosting in old cedars
their tails hanging
long
as the hair of Absalom.

Two by the doors of the old hall
feathered fans outstretched
shimmering seas reflecting
on the wall rainbows.
Warriors in their ancient dance
displaying, thrumming, vibrating
until their feathers sang
and the grass trembled.

Later
as the moon rose on the lawns beyond
seafoam
white peacocks bowing and turning
taut as temple dancers
churning the night with mournful cries,
Dido's song of farewell.

FLORA AND FAUNA

It was the sun glistening, catching
the twist on the small horns, auger shells,
that first caught my attention.

His back against an ancient beech, sitting
almost hidden behind tall bracken
quietly watching through the fronds.
You said, how this must be
an autumn to remember, such intense
colour, the woods scarlet, amber,

burnt honey, burnished copper, all
against such clear blue skies
and this the middle of November.

I looked again, but couldn't find him,
only the gentle rustling of a small breeze
moving the branches, gold arrows

leaves shimmering, dipping in the sun,
shadows of leaves on the trunks of trees
hidden by the great oak he is still there.

You said, you saw a fawn, a pricket
perhaps a young buck in his second year,
all was the same, sunlight, the colour,

the woods, birds calling, but something other
those small horns, a faun surely
Pan enjoying the last of the autumn weather…

fred

three of us, the woman in the garden
and the two of us

the two of us don't move
too much

a water lily bud could be one of us
the way the point breaks above water, tight

noses the air,
the woman in the garden calls me fred

how she jumps, throws up her arms
when the two of us

leap high into the rushes
plop back into darkness

best is when I croak, on warm nights
I croak the stars down, watch them

tumble, each popping green,
brown bubbles bursting is one of us

my skin hangs clammy
motionless I sit for hours

feel the silence enter me, enter us
then splash.

CAT

He comes and goes as he pleases,
in and out of our gardens
sometimes, sunning himself on a roof,
on a wall, a black three legged cat.

Nobody knows who owns him
nobody knows where he lives.
Watering the garden in the cool of the evening
I never saw him in the shadows of the greenhouse;

someone, sometime, must have let loose
a cannon of water full on him,
whatever is cat terror burned in his being
for, as he saw me, hose in hand gently

watering my neighbours hanging flower baskets,
he became hexed into a nightmare, became
a black rapidly revolving vortex, a whirling
spinning catherine wheel inside that greenhouse

unaware of the open door, as a bullet, no
rocket, he hurled himself
head first through the side panes of glass
exploding in shards of glittering splintered stars

he disappeared, no trace of blood, just
vanished, leaving me gasping, left
to explain, the sudden summer frost covering
the grass, my neighbour's shattered greenhouse.

Today, a week since that disaster,
       I saw him, sunning himself on the back wall,
not a care in his cat world,
but then, he can't be a black three legged cat for nothing...

THE JUDAS DEER

This stillness that is midnight
too early yet, these stealthy men
they need the hours that claim the dying
it is their waiting game.

Silent the woods, dark
you don't see King James's deer
their sleek black coats slide into shadows
but there, an albino, light shining in the night
a Judas deer who goes before
who draws the killers to the herd

a deer you could mistake for a unicorn.
So now we cull the white
to spare the herd
and our woods are poorer
for the loss of magic.

MOON STRUCK

Surrounded as I am
by deer, by badger
by small wild things,
fox and stoat
moon circles my cottage.
Pale puffball, goat's beard
dandelion clock in the blue morning sky
grounds me as a loadstone,
yet, as a lodestar I soar.

RANA TEMPORARIA

As if a hand
had torn
not bread, but part
of a watery autumn sun
thrown it, pale among the leaves,

a large yellow frog, so
satisfied he seemed
his apple skin bulging, pulsing
a frog who would a wooing go
needing no kiss.

When frogs are croaking
expect rain,
these last few days
rain has fallen in cascades
clogging all drains.

The top road flooded,
some say
frogs fell from the skies
perhaps a water spout
sucked up a pond
and down fell frogs.

One summer long ago
lying on the grass
I peered into the hollow
at the base of an ancient oak
in that darkness
two eyes peered back at me.

I can't remember now, toad or frog
only shock as our eyes held each other.

This summer the garden heaved with baby frogs
so quick they moved, so far they jumped,
surely, not these the plagues of Egypt?

Swarms of flies, pestilence, boils, gnats
blood, hail, locusts, darkness
death of the first born, I understand all these
but not homely, golden as a Pitmaston pine apple
garden frogs.

THREE

Betty Brown was dark
Pretty, sharp and sly
Joan had a white puffy face
Small black shoe-button eyes.
They were my tormentors
at my first school
The little place
At the bottom of the hill.

Betty Brown would
Put her arm around me
Smile, then pinch me.
Joan never smiled
She would stare hard
Then pinch me.

I tried not to sit near them
But they always found me
Betty Brown
And her friend Joan.

WATER LILY

Crushed between his fingers, such a small fragment
limp as her small body, face down, arms spread
as a water lily, as if she were watching fish far
below, but floating

a fragment from her dress how? He did not know,
he should have tried harder to catch her running
so alive through the grasses, her laughter lost
in the sound of rooks returning in the evening.

Daddy watch me, watch me, he hears her in the rain
in the wind, in the leaves, Daddy watch me
he hears her in the sound of traffic, watch me
in the steam of the kettle, the scratching
of birds in the eaves early,

Emily aged seven, Emily of those strong limbs
fingers beginning to change from little child
to girl but never woman,
hands eager for making music, for drawing.

Eyes not grey, a hint of blue as his Norfolk skies
like the sheen on the lake.
In the sound of the rooks he had not heard the splash
as his daughter floated

caught not by his hands, caught in the end by reeds,
holding her close to warm her, not believing what his eyes
what his heart told him, keening her name, rocking
backwards and forwards, with the rooks calling.

Now in the cool of evening he walks this path
through the long grasses, remembering,
his new neighbour by the lake fishing, unknowing,
looks up smiling, hearing the rooks.

DENDROCOPOS MAJOR - **THE GREAT SPOTTED**

A woodpecker ready for the harlequinade
rests in the apple tree,
some call him the rain bird
and yes, tomorrow's forecast is for showers.

A court jester in his cap and bells
glorious amongst birds,
he's had his fill of insects, nuts
from the cage that hangs from the tree.

The small birds hold back, wait,
then slow and undulating, in bounds he is gone
his colours
flashing pennants against the April sun.

INTERWEAVING

His voice was quiet
"that is clear, and that"
I saw or rather the camera showed
a beautiful flower so like
an under water anemone
its petals stinging tentacles.
"What part of my anatomy is that?"
"That" said the surgeon "is your problem."

We come into this world alone
alone we leave it
as passing flowers or fragrance of flowers
we touch, or are touched,
but mostly, as we pass, alone.

Tares, thistles, goosegrass generous
with its small burrs, cling to our hair, our clothes
bindweed snares, clasps our feet
nettles scorch our hands, still we persist,
in spite of weeds we garden
indifferent to chilling frosts
or gales that fell old beeches.

Once, as a child I watched my mother
on a winter's street collapse
as a whisper, silently as a pack of cards
or beech or grass before the scythe.

As a mad bull, last night, the wind
gusting and snorting, without warning
felled the great beech,
branches like tangled hair floating
on the grass, on the flooded road.

Official men from Highways and Byways
have cleared the road for traffic,

from the cottages unofficial men, logging
stacking, nothing wasted, firewood for next winter.

Wild garlic will spread its pale fingers
its white flowers, mounds of slender green
will cover wounds, jagged scars, in time
bluebells mantle torn earth.

In the stillness that follows turmoil
is the wonder,
 the interweaving
the ant with cyclamen, woodlouse with the wood
seed with flower, we no different.
'In my beginning is my end'

OUTING

If it wasn't Horner Waters
it was on the way
under the overhang of trees

silence louder than waves on the rocks,
upside down stars, pebbles
glinting beneath water

earth smells, snail trails
crumpled cheeks of moss
harts tongue, greenness of light

shadow of light, shadings
on tree trunks on oaks,
shock cold the water

as unexpected pain
lapping stepping stones

small whirlpools
sucking bare white feet
easy to slide

deeper, become shadow
arm into branch,
hair into weed,
fingers, small minnows

tongue, the flower of honeysuckle
eyes, the scream of hare,
stealth of stoat.

UNDERWATER

Walking these beechwoods
is to walk underwater.
As far as I can see
mists of bluebells,
         growth you almost hear
purling of birds, as smoke
deer disappear in the shadow of trees,
nothing disturbs this underwater
stillness.
Time replaced by scent, easy
to slip out of balance
float into luminous particles
drift beneath green lace,
         walking these beechwoods.

After e e cummings

In soft rain
warm as new milk, the sea

jelly fish pulsate, pass
transparent as lost ghosts,

under the pier, seaweed
sways as young girl's hair

waves wash gently, softly
suck, spew shingle

star fish, razor fish
scattered spoils on wet sand

here are all our beginnings
it is always ourselves we find in the sea.

REMEMBERING

Sounds of the sea, of the shingle beach,
footsteps at night crunching pebbles,
smell of tar, feel of tar
of wrack, of marram grass swaying, hiding
children playing.

Boom of fog horn,
small fingers knitting
knitting scarves, knitting
balaclava helmets for men,
the lightship sea tossing.

Watching at night, light wash
my bedroom walls white
lulling me to sleep.

Sand gardens, sand castles, sand
in our sandwiches, between toes
under finger nails, in our bed sheets.

Under the pier, our knitted swimsuits
brown and yellow as bees
hung out to dry, baggy to our knees,
rock, pink and white, sticky and sweet,
rock pools to cool our feet
crabs to catch, star fish, me
wanting to be a mermaid.

HOLLY TREES

Slender hands raised in prayer
stand tall behind the old tiled barn
scarlet berries light a grey November day.
A small breeze sways the trees
birds on every branch fly up, fly down
as sparks on a winter fire.
Shadows lengthen, steal across the wall
before darkness clothes the cottages
into forgetfulness, leaving night
to the creatures of the night
to stoat, to badger, and the hunting owl.

POPLARS

Always the poplars,
from her windows of the tall Victorian house
there they were, two of them, slender
holding up her sky, tremulas,
higher than apple, lilac, higher
than trees in all other gardens
they filled her space, her eyes
dominated her world.

After the war
she tried to find the house, nothing remained
even roads were changed
only the hill was the same
the poplars erased,
she too seemed to have no existence
she had become a girl in someone else's dream.

LIKE TEETH IN A SKULL

Three jagged oak trees
in a circle
bleached white as bone
not the Skeleton Coast
but here in an English shire
their arms outstretched
against a cornflower sky
as if in a ritual dance
a rain dance
for our planet.

MIDSUMMER'S EVE

The garden creeps closer
concealing the cottage
one becomes the other
hollyhocks inside the porch
honeysuckle peers through windows
jasmine clings to walls.

The air cumbered by birds
with the swish of their wings
swift shadows skim roofs
pass over grass, tonight the moon is full
            tomorrow summer solstice
            so much fecundity I could drown.

Out of nine blossoms
was Blodeuwedd born
primroses for wantonness
flowers of oak, flowers of broom
meadowsweet, cockle the devil sowed,
bean blossoms for little ghosts

nettle, chestnut, thorn
nine powers for nine flowers,
long and white her fingers
as the ninth wave of the sea.
On this day of days, to drown in flowers
in the fluting of birds, call of owl
listen,   ask for no more.

CONSIDER THE LILIES OF THE FIELD

It is my flowers, so generous
each month, through the year something fresh
not just content to grow, they slowly devour my cottage
munching their way to my door.

Back and front jasmine and honeysuckle
creeping through windows.
Lathyrus grandiflorus that old thug of a cottager's pea
pushes through floorboards
but it is glorious drowning in nature.

On one side woods stretching
dark and cool heavy in silence, in deer, in badger.
On the other, meadows, fat with woolly white sheep
and in the sky more woolly white sheep of clouds.

At night, foxes pass beneath my window
I have the moon and stars to lull me to sleep
as a small wooden rowing boat rocks on the waters,
birds wake me with their song
fluting of blackbird, trill of robin.

Who said give me a small house
one fruit tree, a pool of sweet water
and I shall live in blissful solitude,
I do,   I do,   I do.

A CHAPLET

Five herbs for healing
five for protection.
Cleavers, Barberry
root of Dandelion
Marigold and Horsetail.
Bitter for shriving, bitter
as anguish, as sloes, as unexpected pain.
In deepest winter
a cluster of snails hold fast, tight
as a grenade beneath leaves,
snowdrop bayonets pierce the earth.
We find our own epiphany,
mine I hold
in a chaplet of herbs.

LADY IN THE STRAW

Remember love,
I'd gather scented rushes
strew them on the floor
our trundle bed
woven with much skill and care
with small rush you plaited me my ring
look love, the token I gave you
a sprig of heather, head of corn, a jay's bright feather.
Some say a rush ring is a thing to scorn
not me my dove.
Our roof of reeds you said would last for fifty years
it had the sheen of a mute swan's egg
and so it has my love.
For bread we never had to beg
a skip for bees, a small milch cow, but more
we had each other.
That was then and this is now
this aching cold, this loneliness, this empty corner chair,
I won't forget love
I was your lady in the straw.

EARTH

What I remember most
as a child
was the colour of the earth.
When it rained
when the gullies filled
when the water ran off the fields
they ran with blood.
Here in the east
it is flint country
sky the colour
of sparrows' eggs.
Stones multiply by night
soil shallow over chalk
veiled by traveller's joy
false blossoms.
Smell the smell of earth
nothing rings truer
a mellowness
haunted by jonquil
by winter sweet
but always stranger, stronger
the scent of death in hawthorn flowers.

One of the *Graeae*

born white haired
but I have all my teeth
both my eyes.

On the edge
as sea thrift clings to cliff
wondering when
how long, if?

How many dandelion clocks
left to blow
stars to count
pebbles to feel, to clutch

shall I know?
Until then
breathe, thankful

for slender stalks of crocus grass
pushing through moist earth
for the pierce of a thorn to show I live.

OUT OF TUNE

How do I draw down the threads
to weave a poem
when I sing out of tune?

Easier to find the source of a stream,
I hold no diviner's rod, no willow wand
to catch a dream.

My head is full of whispers, of almosts
of what might have been.
Old sepia photographs of what was once
tomorrow.

Was I good at anything?
Made beautiful babies though,
sang lullabies, out of tune
out of tune all my life.

With flowers you know where you are
a dandelion is always a dandelion, never a rose
parsley is always parsley, but with a man, who knows?

It's safe in my garden, everything grows,
cities unnerve me, too many strangers all closed.

I shall plant tulips to spill, splattered
like a bucket of water upturned,
colour to feast the eyes, scents to feast the soul.

I paint with my plants and with words
yet, sadly still out of tune.

KALENDS

January brings the Disting moon

Sweetness of honey, of lily of the valley
flowers of mahonia scent my kitchen,
outside winter holds the garden,
small blotched ghosts of apples
on naked branches, wizened fruits
hang like glass baubles, shattered
on a forgotten Christmas tree:
birds criss-cross the grass, snowdrops
aconites feast my eyes.

From aching limbs
from chilling blasts
Sweet One deliver us...

February fill-dyke
of all the months in the year
curse a fair Fevrueer.

No rain, but sun so warm
winter is upended
Candlemas is now
Midsummer's Eve, sun
shines hot on leafless
trees, primroses scorched,
burnt brown my violet leaves
no water in the pond.

Sweet One,
send rain, send seasons
in their turn...

*March the month of Iduna
bearer of the magic apples.*

The rains have come
a shimmer of green, shadows
the old apple tree, puddles
lie on the grass, dried up
rivers run again, rain
filling ditches, forgotten
fords reclaiming lanes, sky
so close to earth,
no beginning no end
moisture slippery as a caul.

*From sudden flood
from frozen spring
Sweet One deliver us...*

When that April with his showers soote...

Rape is in flower
fields of bitter yellow
beneath a purple sky
clouds bruised, swollen
by rain, hedgerows snaking
the lane, heaving under
fresh enamelled leaves,
frogspawn simmering
in the pond, wild cherry
nets the woods in lace.
Gardens embraced by birdsong
by brimstone butterflies
air so sharp in scent
it blows my senses,
earth sings
and the Greenman
dances to her tune.

From nibbling muntjac
from gall mites
from eelworms
Sweet One deliver us...

Phyllida with gardens gay
was made the Lady of the May

In the woods
the scent of bluebells,
in the garden
for one week
the tree peony flowers.
Frost bites at night
snails and slugs
young lettuce plants
devour.

From these last evils
Sweet One deliver us...

June brings tulips, lilies, roses…

All day the cuckoo calls,
green beans twine
through tripods
of grey willows, plump
scented rose buds, their
petals expand, water cans
brimming, rest in shadow
below angelica stars.
Winds come from the north east
battering flowers, bruising
all soft growth,
rain churning trackways,
small puffs of cumulus
sheep clouds, dot
sodden hillsides.
Yan tan thethera pethera pimp
bumfit is 15, 20 is figgit,
figgit plump fleece chewing the cud,
fields of corn flattened;
in the garden
red lily beetle
reeks destruction.

*From gales
from red lily beetle
Sweet One deliver us…*

*Hot July brings cooling showers
apricots and gillyflowers.*

From the arched gateway
hang stars of white jasmine
at night foxes bark
echoing wolves;
a family of peacocks
the hen creamy as dough
the cock glints jewels,
greens, blues, gold,
three buff chicks walk the walls
perch on the apple tree, fly
to the safety of the long grass;
in the fields black faced sheep
in the garden fat orange marigolds
where the cat lies dozing in the sun.

*From pismire
from sudden storms
Sweet One deliver us...*

Lammas-tide
pale moon doth rain
red moon doth blow.

Orange is the August moon
fox-tailed the fields,
newly ploughed meadows
earth prised open, fields
smouldering embers, in this
haze of heat.
In the cottage an eight eyed
eight legged spider
suspended half way up the wall,
webs garland the mornings.
Never slight the Gods,
poor Arachne changed forever
to a spider.
Fat plums in the garden
hedges of parsley.

From earwigs
from hairy caterpillars
Sweet One deliver us…

September blow soft
till the fruit's in the loft.

Drought in September
such heat at noon
not even the cat
ventures out, butterflies
bask on hot stones,
at night
stars bright on the breath
of a clear sky, stirrings
of autumn, owls call
the scream of a hare
ivy circles the moon.

From sawfly
from codlin moth
Sweet One deliver us...

October.
**The hart loves the high wood
the hare loves the hill.**

Tawny apples lattice the sky,
noonday shadows cast dark
fingers over freckled furrows
more flint than soil, as if
earth gave up not her dead
but skylark eggs;
beside the gate, rose heps
brush feathers of fireweed,
on the horizon a tractor
the size of a child's toy.
Now is the time for pumpkin
lanterns to light our doors
for Halloween, hard frost
at night, in the woods deer
are rutting.

*From bogles
from things
that go bump
in the night
Sweet One deliver us...*

November brings the blast
Wayland the smith fashions his anvil.

Shrouded and silent the garden
leaves still hang on the oak
pale as a faded silk shawl.
In the pantry puddings wait
trim in their calico, ready
for the Christmas feast;
a blackbird with one white wing
tugs a fat worm from the grass,
by the door winter jasmine
in flower,
a fountain of yellow stars.

From leaky roofs
from all agues
Sweet One deliver us...

A green Christmas, a fat churchyard,
of all the trees in the greenwood
the holly bears the crown.

No bleak midwinter this,
a strange solstice
no milk comes frozen
home in pail, fog masks
the moon, by day the sun
flowers bloom where frost
should lie, yet comes more
rain, more nesting birds
a summer's progress
in the very dead of winter
birth or death?
There was a birth certainly,
hang up the holly, rosemary
and bay, garland the ivy
count the berries
on the mistletoe,
the line is there
before we draw it…

From lightning
from falling planets
Sweet One, deliver us…

FINDING LOVE

I never found my love
not for the want of looking
perhaps I searched too far, too long
for what I looked for was always wrong.

I made a charm on St Valentine's eve
I placed my shoes like a letter T
in hopes my true love I should see.

I never found my love
not for the want of looking,
I searched up hills, I searched in dales
looking, always looking.

Too strong his spell was cast on me
so many times I thought he'd come,
to find he was not as I thought he would be
obvious to all, but not to me.

I never found my love
not for the want of looking,
up in the air, down in the sea
while all the time he was waiting for me.

I had expected a young man you see
not bent and old and grey as me
I still place shoes shaped in a T
in hopes my true love I shall see.

I watched the hearse draw through the town
I thought how sad some love has gone
unknown, it carried you from me
dust covers now shoes shaped in a T.

SHAPE SHIFTER

I thought I saw a hare, by the church
              crossing my path and off across the fields
so fast, but it was a black rabbit
with large ears.
Fishermen never mention hares
rather remain ashore all day should they but see one.
In pain hares scream
grind their teeth in warning.
                        Once every witch had her familiar
a cat or a hare, shape shifters.
More often now a hare to hide his scent
will shelter under junipers, it confuses hounds and foxes.

TREES

There is a stirring in the trees
when the west wind blows,
the old sit peacefully in their shade
children climb, dream,
but at night
watch the shadows slip silent along the wall.

Trees belong to night
hold their own council
know no time but growth.

Ancient these yews who knew the Weird
tall and dark, knew the White Lady
who walked the woods, deathly pale
her lips red as holly berries,
when trees walked,
when Blodeuwedd, lady made of flowers
was turned to owl.

In autumn with the turning of the leaves,
burnt umber, chrome yellow, sienna
firecracker scarlet, there comes a silence
past and present merge, time slips sideways
it is not the blackbird's fluting you can hear
but music far more ancient.

RINGSHALL

For two days now
they have hardly
left each other

all through yesterday's
heavy rain, side by side
almost merging into one

this morning, they are dancing
pirouetting, now together
now apart, acrobats balancing

trembling on telephone wires
their circus top the sky,
collared doves, on the cusp of summer.

WHEELER END

Vast expanse of sky, clouds
long, rolling as sea breakers
red kite, soaring, sweeping
climbing, dipping, twisting
hovering,
sailing the clouds, swifter
than wind,
circling tirelessly, their long wings,
bent backwards in flight, forked tail
space Vikings.

TOBIAS HAD HIS ANGEL

For D.H. Lawrence
the god Hermes sat by his hearth,
for m.r. peacocke
a vagrant stripling god
difficult to tell from groundsel,
bittercress, or burdock kind
but he left his print in flattened buttercups.
For me, the smallest robin
a master magician who greets
me at my gate
who never takes his final bow.
On matchstick legs he darts
from bush to tree, knows
whose garden fork turns up the fattest worm.
Today, a hand's breadth away,
perched low on a branch,
his eyes round obsidian stars,
he sang so clear a song,
in that small moment it held the universe.

SWIFTLY COMES THE SPARROWHAWK

Small white lettuce seeds
tiny as a child's nail parings
plump brown rocket seed
the size of an ant's egg

saved from last year
I hold them in a slip of paper
hoping they will germinate
in this moist earth.

Under the eaves a blackbird's nest
a cup of dry grass, mud and leaves
pulsate with orange beaks
opening wide, eager for food.

In the waxing of the moon,
planting seeds in the warmth of the sun
they grow strong, pricking them out
I place them safe from snails, slugs, birds

in the morning, on the stone path outside
the blackbird's nest spoiled,
soft featherless bodies strewn
among bruised and fallen rose petals.

THIRD HAND

How is it some tools
slip comfortably
into the hand, while
others jar, irritate
cause blisters, splinters
trip you up?

I have a favourite
narrow, slim as a tulip
its scoop no longer glistens
as the morning star,
now speckled, homely as a hen
scratching for grain.

Worn smooth its wooden handle
as an old saddle, colour of cobnut
of warm beer
of crusted brown bread, my garden trowel
to dig small weeds, plant bulbs,
an extension of my fingers into moist earth.

Once we humans cupped, dug earth
with our bare hands,
then a planting stick, or bone
trowels haven't changed since
Adam delved and Eva span.

So small our earth we cannot help
but tread on bones.
In my garden generations have tilled the soil
now I hold back the weeds.
The woods are waiting to return
holly, oak, beech, chestnut.

Outside our garden the wild wood waits
until then
my trowel is about his business
turning earth
         planting seed   searching
                  for Devil's Garters.

WINTER AFTERNOON

A chill breeze from the north
worries frozen leaves,
snow softens the gardens
outlines the apple tree
as a chalk drawing.

Tongues of late afternoon sun
dribble gold on trunks of trees
branches, black arms reaching for a sky
blue as chicory flowers
puffs of corncockle clouds
black seeds of destruction.

Inside a woodfire crackles, flames
throw shadows on old walls,
on an old clock tick-tocking into spring.

EARLY MORNING

Four o'clock, early morning
mist shrouds the garden
air splinters into birdsong

slowly the rose arbour
the old bush roses, ginko
lavender, lad's love, become

more solid, no longer loom
in space as old fishing
smacks homing out of sea fog.

Later, walking the path
to the woods, moons of elder
dog roses star the trees, squirrels

skitter, play last across
on the forest floor, deer
browse undisturbed, yet

I am cobwebbed, stuck, held
firmer than any birdlime, listening
to sounds snared in my head, mostly

I sleep through, perhaps catch one note
this morning, I heard, still hear
this miracle, this gift, the dawn chorus.

FOG

Around the cottages
stealthily creeping
devouring gardens, pressing
hard against panes of glass
fog smothering all it meets.
In this place of shades and shadows
to see against my window
shooting from bare wood
a fountain of stars
more precious than summer flowers
winter jasmine.

WINTER

Dark the woods, dark the trees
as chalk on a school blackboard
snow traces branches,
birds silent search for food
ice holds the earth
even rats are in their holes
yet, in this sea of cold
birds still fly, fly from frozen
bush to bush.
A blackbird scurries down the path
souls so small
how do you survive?
The barn door ajar
some protection from winter's blast.

FORECAST

"Three frosts in a row
then rain."

Softly turns the year
burnished fields of August
now wear a moleskin coat.
Leaves hang honeyed
cinnamon beside the haws,
black fists of elderberries
thrust through hedgerows.
Sheep hug the hill
float in mist.

In the gardens, sprawling
yellow daisies jostle
straddle cottage walls, lope
haphazardly along the lane
to come to rest beside
the lychgate and the yew,
yellow daisies staring
indolently as we pass.

Sensing in the air
the chill of first frost
I remember the farmer's words.

SUMMER

Summer was a cabin by the sea,
small, narrow, painted green
no window, a door open to the beach.
When it rained, when the east wind blew
sand filled our mouths, our hair,
covered shelves, lived in our shoes
salted, peppered all our food.

The sea sucked rocks
clattering them in its mouth
to spill them further along the shore,
until quiet waters lapped six steps
slippery with seaweed that led to the cabin.
All was of the sea, we creatures of the waves
of rock pools, grey satin swept sky
soft as an Orford oyster in its shell.

CHANGE

Always unexpected, the day
you walk into the garden or
open your back door to collect milk
the air has changed, summer
slipping into autumn.

Remember the smell, the excitement
of your new school exercise book,
the coolness, the untouched white paper
clean new sheets, the first flat
shiny conker container of all our childhoods.

Now I become hunter gatherer, searching
for nuts, berries, sticks, wood
for winter fires, horder of food
chutney maker, jelly maker, preparing
for a winter two overcoats cold.

Mornings cobweb hung, leaves, plants
glistening, trembling with puckered stars
earth moss soft, moist underfoot, silvered trails
of snails cover the path, but it is the air that sings,
sings the old song of what is to come.

YESTERDAY

Nature's caul hung drab as uncooked faggots
encasing all in a clenched soggy ball,
today, amazingly the air needle sharp, sun
illuminating every cranny of my room
of the November garden, even the gravel path
shining sea clean.

A slight breeze moves drooping blooms of hollyhock
but in the sky, birds criss-cross at such speed
black angels, barbed arrows, pierce the sun.

GRAVEL GARDENS

How dismayed you'd be John Clare,
through ignorance, desire for more
we are despoiling nature,
mountains strewn with rubbish
seas polluted, air polluted, soil polluted.

Silence a scarce commodity
wilderness difficult to find
how have we destroyed so much?

In our new world of global warming
no place for hollyhocks to grow,
cowslips, violets, the scent of roses
where have our water-meadows gone?
In gravel gardens flowers are grasses.

Orpheus turned beggar, Pan a displaced person.

We hand our children and our children's children
a toxic dried up globe
drought, famine, war, destruction
                              where no bird sings.

POST CARD FROM THE ABYSS

No stars, no moon. a hard place this, darkness
has swallowed our earth, eaten our crops
taught us to walk tall on bleeding feet
our bellies swollen.
Day has become night, night the harshness of scavengers.
Lanes awash with melt water, paths lost rivers, meadows
crumble into the sea.
Our children weigh so little, they might
take fright as birds, small souls who slip so easily
through our fingers, our hands, gasping for life.

DECEMBER 2nd 1984

They ran, not knowing where to go
as ants, whose nest has been destroyed.
Fortunate the few who never woke to know such sorrow.
per nostra crimina.

As Thuggee in the night the killer came,
stench of rotting cabbage over a city hung
no warning, yet so many souls were slain.
per nostra crimina.

Corporate greed from where the eagle flies
'am I my brother's keeper?' is the song they sang
from the land of the free, of hominy grits, of apple pies.

You who speak of freedom, who fly the flag
have long since closed your minds, your birthright sold
for a mess of pottage. Thirty silver pieces for a body bag.
per nostra crimina.

Destroyer of illusions, Siva, were you witness?
Lungs in unbearable pain, a warning muted
toxic sludge ten feet high creates more sickness.
per nostra crimina.

In polluted soil no seed will grow.
Cain stalks the land of Nod.
Twenty three years ago, they ran, not knowing where to go.
per nostra crimina.

LE CHAT BLANC
(a cat on a postcard)

Everything is elongated, my hand,
fingers can brush the ceiling
lying flat on my bed my toes
can push the end wall of my room,

trees reach the moon, branches sweep the sky
hang like lank hair, rest in the grass,
shadows never end, circle the globe, corset earth.

I haven't seen an elongated cat, until today
friendly and smiling, a smarm of marmalade
smear of tortoiseshell, mangled quite flat

see how his fine tail sways, how he holds it high,
Le Chat Blanc, not in anger, not spitting
as cats do,

a benign smile on his face, as if to say
hey, look, I too can stretch, touch
most ceilings, fish the darkest pools

swish goes his tail, swish my fingers,
I part the air, I touch his whiskers
this cat can dance, bounce off the moon
this *chat blanc.*

HELIX ASPERSA

You are not welcome
each morning, there across my stone floor
a silver trail, not one
more like Euston Station's marshalling yard
how you get in baffles me
unless you squeeze through ventilating bricks.
I've seen snails on top floor window panes,
don't ask me how,
snails or great fat slugs as whales.
In the garden is bad enough
yet, why does it touch me so,
finding in winter under leaves or stone
a great ball of snails holding fast
one to another, reminding me
of finely carved ivory Japanese rat-balls.
If I could cast a spell, would I send you packing?
Let my slippers rub away your silver trails.

A PROLIFERATION OF PIGS

of rumps, trotters, ears, squeals
honks, snouts, young fat and pink,
a heaving mass, no beginning no end

an eruption of bacon, of pork
squishing, squirming, squashing
clambering one over the other

up down and up again, six pigs
twelve pigs a moving mass
quivering quadrupeds questing
piggery in tumultuous motion   marvellous.

GARDENING FOR WORDS

Swaying in the breeze a winding shroud
fine as gossamer, the palest chrysalis
spun on a nettle leaf, while I struggle
pulling, teasing out words that
for the most part, hide.

I try to write a poem, all evaporates
before it is even formed,
watching morning glory twine so tight
covering bamboo poles, to burst
into trumpets of blue and mauve so radiant

it makes me breathless, no problem
for the honeysuckle who flings her arms
in such abandon on any host and grows

why me, why so inadequate, inadequate
the garden murmured, trees bend down
their branches whispering in the grass
inadequate they breathe, why bother if words
don't fall as rain, or flutter, homing in
as doves, all has been said before, far better

yet, you find me here waiting, wanting
to write a poem, so I potter in the garden
sow seeds in the greenhouse, but never
in my mind,   that alas lies fallow.

HOBBY HORSE

Sent into Somerset
from a city hung in elephants
soft grey barrage balloons
criss-crossing a winter sky,
a city of sandbagged trenches
gas masks, the blackout,
a frightened child who couldn't cry
who watched the Thames on fire.

I can't remember now
just when it was, was it May?
I remember the white thatched cob cottages
the small town by the sea
the harbour wall, the crowds, two men
under a spotted canvas skin.

The great horse's wooden head
eyes that rolled, a scarlet tongue that lolled,
the wild horse prancing, menacing, dancing
we children screaming, half in terror, half wanting
to be caught,
somewhere a pipe and drum, a fiddle playing.

A WOOD IN LATE NOVEMBER

Painted with care, long black brush strokes
calligraphy,
an invitation to a firing of a wood kiln.

Deep in the forest
a track leads to a cottage
to a Japanese potter, to his painter wife.

It is raining, mist hides the valley
all day soft rain has fallen
soft as a haar from the sea.

On this hill are ancient trees, are tumuli,
birds silent, deer nowhere to be seen
only the dry, drip of the leaves

moisture seeping into shoes, down necks
sparkling our clothes, we stand in groups
strangers waiting, drawn by the potter's clay
unable to move, cold to the bone.

The potter, his long hair wet to his scalp,
a small thick-set man, checks his fire's heat
his heart's passion.

Shaman or showman, he opens the door of his kiln
in the darkness of the late afternoon, the fire glows
bright as the core of the sun.

He puts on gloves, takes long-handled pincers,
St Dunstan when he tweaked the Devil's nose,
reaches from the fire, beakers, pots, bowls

these he places on a shelf of stone
as they cool they change their colours
sing, each pot sings, nightingales in a Chiltern wood
or angels, summoning the Magi.

GREEN GARLANDS

Beautiful in her smallness
soft as an April shower,
skin supple as a silk glove
plump to her long tail
curled as a crescent moon,
her hair hangs loose, cowls
her shoulders, flowers
garland her head
her breasts quilled daisies
childlike she peers into her mirror
as petals of primrose of heartsease
speedwell and strawberry leaves
tumble about her.

I found her in the margin
of an old gardening book, when
sow thistles and colewort
were grown for the pot, almost
forgotten, a mouse woman.

GREEN MAN

I the voice in the green
flute eared, mouse tongued
garlands once hung on my arms
feet pounded the earth
the circle dance at dawn.

Through smoke of hawthorn blossom
by the still black pool where deer
and badger pass, I watch, eyes
glinting through leaves.

Ivy my hair, pipistrelles my hands
flowers by beard, frogs, snails, toads
grass snakes my feet.

They carved me in oak, gagged
bound me, placed me safe
below the misericord. Kept close
by lock and bolt. One midsummer's eve
the door ajar, one heave and I stepped out.

Earth shakes, milk curdles, the moon is red.
I the voice in the green, I the thunder
I the rain, I conjure, stalking
straddling the woods in moonshine
I sing in the scream of the hare.

A COTTAGE GARDEN

All is disorder,
plants twine, prop each other up,
beans climb willow tripods, grow
beside Madonna lilies, rose, herbs,
toads live undisturbed, fox visits nightly.

Honeysuckle, yellow as best farm butter, creamy
as beestings, feastings for hawkmoth, struts the porch.
Close by the stone step, five petalled pinks fade
as a bruised and painted sun.

Hairy bumblebees, wings transparent as etched glass
wear yellow stripes of burly rugby players.
Lusting satin black hollyhocks open wide for hoverflies
for wasps and bees, flowers ornate as buckles
on silk high-heeled shoes.

Scarlet damselflies in tandem, scents, shadows, lure you
deeper where the path is lost, now all is enchantment
nothing is as it seems.
Look a leaf, no a comma's pinking sheer wings that are closed,
in mist, slender grasses become young girls' fine hair
snood-caught, sparkling.

White flowers belong to the moon, see them at early dawn
little ghosts dew heavy.
Sprawled beside the gate, blue-eyed alkanet, its large pointed
leaves cat-tongue rough, grasp all who enter.

In this garden nothing sleeps, even under snow
in soil leaf-mould rich bulbs push upwards.
For mouse, for shrew this is a fearful time, owl is hunting,
stoat slips silent across the path, night pulsates with eyes.

IN SILENCE I FOUND HER

A dark cloak about her
an oak tree of a woman
the fast river beside her
her voice is the greenwood
her staff a green willow
her cell empty of clutter
lay woman unlettered
many have sought her
few turn from her door
the larks they are singing
the bells they are pealing
all shall be well
and all manner of thing
shall be well.

PEELING AN ONION

1.

Peeling an onion slowly
removing its transparent skins,
thinking of this morning in the market

a reflection of a woman in a window,
something familiar,
surprised she realised it was herself.

We become our mothers, men
their fathers, an expression, tilt of the head,
how far back goes this family face?

We carry hidden layers
curtained interiors we hide behind,
for fear of being bruised, the hurt of love.

2.

She watched the tiny pearls, spilled
mercury slide over the floor
from the broken barometer, pools
of liquid mirrors, breaking and reforming
impossible to catch
as clouds on a windy day, or smoke,

or words, she was finding words hard to hold,
not making sense, fear of not
being understood, reminding her
of standing on the edge of a cliff
seeing below the froth of sea-foam breaking
on to rocks, the froth in a glass of barley wine.

> *'The water is wide I can not get o'er,*
> *and neither have I wings to fly;*
> *give me a boat that will carry two*
> *and both shall row, my love and I ...'*

3.

Once as a little girl, she thought
she could walk on water,
she and her best friend, slipped
quietly from the boarding house;

a summer night, unnoticed
they sat on the harbour wall,
watched the fat full moon
cast a path across the water,

daring each other, holding hands
they walked the moonlit path.
Wet, shivering, stinking of wrack
they climbed the fire escape, safe
into school, a boarding house humming
as a hive of angry bees.

Do we try to pass into that other space
or is it other time, familiar but altered?
Like growing old, unaware until
you catch yourself reflected, you
but not you, mother, grandmother?

> *'You gave me a mantle for to wear*
> *lined with grief and stitched with care ...'*

4.

She thought again of the iris,
all winter she had waited to see it bloom
early in summer it flowered,
palest blue as the June sky
she marvelled at its texture, watched
the plump blooms open one by one,
startled by the sparrowhawk, clumsily
she dropped her secateurs, breaking the slender stem
flowers bruised and broken lay on the earth,
swifter than love is lost, or a head
laid upon a shoulder that leaves the heart ragged.

> *'For love grows old and waxes cold*
> *and fades away like morning dew ...'*

Nothing she could do but wait for another summer
when hedges are filled with wild parsley
and the moon hangs low over the fields.

5.

Summers came, spun out, spent
as flowers of scarlet pimpernel
that close their eyes against the rain,
summers of wild strawberries,
of briars barbed, scars hard to heal.

> *'She set her back against an oak*
> *thinking he was a trusted tree*
> *but first he bent, then he broke ...'*

All her life she sang one song,
never was a good judge of men, chose
the off-beat, the out of tune
but variations on the same theme.

'Give it time, give it time
the grass that was trodden underfoot
it will rise,
oh the willow it will bend
and the willow it will twine ...'

Searching, for what she never found
until, grandchildren filled her arms,
weighed down her hands, her hungry lap,
then such a loving she had never known ...

'She knew not if she sank or swam ...'

MAY MORNING

Sky vole grey,
soft rain falls
as faded blooms of wisteria,
small breeze worries leaves

more birds than flowers,
doves, blackbird, thrush,
petals float from apple blossom
dark shadows, birds skim

pass swiftly over grass,
a woodpecker, pecks at nuts
swings on a metal feeder
hung from a branch;

all is of promise
even the sun creeps from clouds
barely enough blue
to patch a Dutchman's trousers,

birdsong flutes the air
air with hauntings
of frost
on this, the cusp of summer.

ST BRENDAN'S ROWING BOAT

Always the journey back to the sea
to long green seaweed hair
draped over battered wooden groynes
mussel sharp, slipping deeper and deeper
sea now over me, not cold
but breast-warm, above me on marshmallow cliffs
sea thrift in bloom,
caves smudges of black pansies
boom with high water,
blue sky dotted with fat white islands
I can almost touch,
gently swaying, safe in old St Brendan's rowing boat.

BLUE TIT

Always unexpected
a feathered ball of blue and yellow
clings to the lead on my window pane
pecks at the glass, peers into my room
never stays long

never long enough
for me to catch him in a photograph
however patiently I sit and wait,
he's there and then he's gone
a game we play together.